Prepositional Heaven

Prepositional Heaven

Thomas Rabbitt

RIVER CITY PUBLISHING
Montgomery, Alabama

Copyright © 2001 by Thomas Rabbitt. All rights reserved under International and Pan-American Copyright Conventions. Published in the United States by River City Publishing LLC, 1719 Mulberry St., Montgomery, AL 36106.

Library of Congress Cataloging-in-Publication Data

Rabbitt, Thomas, 1943-
Prepositional heaven : poems / by Thomas Rabbitt.
  p. cm.
  ISBN 0-913515-20-5
  1. Tuscaloosa (Ala.)—Poetry. 2. East Harwich (Mass.)—Poetry. 3. Tuam (Ireland)—Poetry. I. Title.
  PS3568.A22 P7 2001
  811'.54—dc21
        2001003452

Designed by Lissa Monroe.
Manufactured by Vaughan Printing in the United States of America.

River City publishes fiction, nonfiction, poetry, children's books, and art. With our cover illustrations we recognize and celebrate the bond between literature and the visual arts. This book's cover art, "Stone Man," is the work of Barbara Kline. To request our catalog or order any of our books, including Thomas Rabbitt's previous volume, Enemies of the State, *phone us at 1 (334) 265-6753. Also visit our web site at www.rivercitypublishing.com.*

Acknowledgments

Some of the poems included here have appeared elsewhere, some in earlier versions. The author is grateful to these publishers and editors for their kind support.

"The Word from Marathon," "Her Widowed Look," "Greek Revival Ghost," "In the Locust Grove," "Home on the Range," "Echolalia," "Salt Water Taffy," "The Capon Islands' News," "Two Lips to Die For," "Orpheus at the River," "Indian Summer in the Capon Islands," "The Division of Fire," "After a Life of Art," "Articles of Faith," "In the Mail," and "Euthanasia" as part of a chapbook, *The Capon Islands' News*, in the *Idaho Review*.

"The House of Dreams," "Opera Queens," "In the Cemetery, Iowa City, Iowa," "The Universal Mall," and "Our Lady of the Vapors" in *The Transfiguration of Dread*, a limited fine arts collection published by Parallel Editions.

"April Fool's Day, Morgan Hall" in *The Black Warrior Review*.

"Snapdragons, Et Cetera" and "Phantom Pain" in *The Distillery*.

"Wren Hunting," "In Eclipse," "Last Will and Testament," and "The Bones of Temple Jarlath" in *The Gettysburg Review*.

"The Cave of the Winds" and "Halloween" in *Shenandoah*.

"Greek Revival Ghost," "Snow Sculpture," and "After a Life of Art" in *Whirligig: A Journal of Language Arts*.

"The Beasts of Coole Park" and "At Columcille's Well" as broadsides from Stillwater Press.

Also by Thomas Rabbitt

Enemies of the State
The Capon Islands' News
The Transfiguration of Dread
Road Kills
The Rehabilitation of Galileo Galilei
The Abandoned Country
The Booth Interstate
Exile

Contents

Foreword
In the Cemetery — 13

Part One—TUSCALOOSA

The Cave of the Winds — 17
After the Flood — 19
When the Devil Drives — 21
In Eclipse — 22
Our Lady of the Vapors — 23
Echolalia — 24
On Convent Street — 25
In the Locust Grove — 26
A Hole in the Ground of Being — 28
The Universal Mall — 29
Phantom Pain — 31
In the Mail — 32
The Teacher Quits — 34
The Word from Marathon — 36
April Fool's Day, Morgan Hall — 37

Part Two—EAST HARWICH

Euthanasia — 41
Dead Skunk — 43
Her Widowed Look — 44
Greek Revival Ghost — 45
Salt Water Taffy — 47

Indian Summer in the Capon Islands	48
On Red River Beach	49
Halloween	50
Sunset Strip	51
After a Life of Art	52
Snow Sculpture	53
The Capon Islands' News	55
Positively Elizabethan	56
Deer in the Headlights	58
Snapdragons, Et Cetera	59

Part Three—TUAM

Beyond Nantucket	63
The Beasts of Coole Park	65
Opera Queens	66
Two Lips to Die For	68
At Columcille's Well	69
When Irish Eyes Are Smiling	71
Articles of Faith	72
Last Will and Testament	74
Orpheus at the River	76
The Bones of Temple Jarlath	77
Home on the Range	79
The House of Dreams	80
The Broken Tower	82
Wren Hunting	85
Sweet Afton	86

Envoi

Epimetheus	91

Foreword

In the Cemetery
—Iowa City, Iowa
Rodina Federova and the Angel of Death

Dead forever, dead under the cast and monstrous grief
Of an angel so black, so tetanic, this praeterite woman
Must be, you think, her lovely moonlight image—you, who call
Rodina *Azrael*, who call the angel *Rodina Federova*,
Sad avenger, on a hillside of rain-washed, wind-worn
Names and numbers, the forever tired, forever dead.
Someone has transfigured her. Today. Someone has
Taken cobbles from a neighbor's grave to smash
Rodina's fingers, crush her toes, bash the modest beauty
From her empty downcast eyes, her lovely folded wings.
Between her last two fingers someone has left a cigarette,
Left the words *take back the night sister spirit dyke*
In purple paint across Rodina's useless human name.
Someone has been more afraid of death than death.
Someone has hoped to turn a few silly words, an image—
Eating out the Angel of Death—into her final victory.
Someone!—foolish enough to smash the mirror in which,
Transcendent, rose the image of her own black dread.

Part One

TUSCALOOSA

The Cave of the Winds

While the entire state of Alabama waits for the latest tornado
To blow over, some of us sit in Papa Boccaccio's wine cellar
And suck up the courage of the evening's breezy convictions.
Meanwhile the wind savagely strips spring's pale innocent leaves
From the saplings the city just planted. Where else might we go
And still pretend we were not intended to die in Tuscaloosa?

In barbaric China a ploughman unearths his Emperor's dream.
Erect in their underground bunkers, handsome clay soldiers await
The invigorating kiss of war. Listen to the drumbeat, the bright fife,
The scream of dying horses. The witch whispers her magic too late
To save us from our dark basement. In the underworld of the afterlife,
This still air of art, we are but clay faces in the Emperor's empty head.

That head, my lord? Cleopatra asks, faced with an important choice.
Good my lord, we are all unplucked fruit. If you depend on me,
May I depend upon whichever head, my lord, it pleases me to choose?
She is fair Egypt, rare desert flower, as cruel as any king, wittier
Than any woman I have ever known. Her game I always lose.
If, like a fool, I listen, will I, while dying, hear the sword's swift voice?

In Eyre Square in Galway City a sculpted poet sits like a lump of wit.
Padraic O'Conaire has won: coldest, curtest, cutest of the Seven Dwarves.
With brazen souls the Irish have their way: the Hags with the Bags,

The Floozie in the Jacuzzi—all art must suck at the witch's tit.
Mad Ireland goes to Disney; so much mad lethal brilliance swerves
To avoid the truth. Yes, Paddy, the public Soul begs in greasy rags.

Most recently in cultured, cluttered Tuscaloosa a bit of statuary rape:
A fascist fountain—a rising pride of eyeless, sexless, hairless boys—
All ass and pectorals—upholding water and a pyramid of one another—
Seducing the eye with flesh, the willing ear with the playful noise
Of falling water—for what we sought to see was ever wet and ripe,
And therefore must be razed to rubble, like one more dead lover.

Maybe tomorrow morning we will wake to find socialist realism
At the cellar door, Marc Antony's head back on his unloved neck,
The bodies of the stone boys in Tuscaloosa still a promise of sin.
If we wake, we are alive. Should we ignore life's minor failures?
Stalin is toothless. The Chinese communes are the glum wreckage
Of intellectual desire. We are still the brilliant clay we burrow in.

After the Flood

Love was not the Charles which, when I was young,
I tried to walk across. I jumped and swam
And my one friend yelled, *I won't rescue you!*
Counterpoint, I thought then. Point, I see now.
I swam back and emerged, covered with mud,
And we went for coffee in Harvard Square.
No one else knew I had done this mad thing
And would do it again in Alabama
The morning after another cold river
Retreated from the Promised Land to leave
Behind such a baptism of surprises:
The riverbank awash in shiny mud
And dying fish which, turning into fossils,
Could look both down on me and up to God.

*

Once I knew a woman who called the park
On River Road the place where failed men walk.
Never the one to turn a phrase or trick—
A ponderous wit—she thought herself really

Too crushing as, indeed, she would have been
Had she, after her last jump, lit upon
Any of the life forms she loved to scorn.
Who could resist? Her splat was so much talk.
Isn't failure whatever spot you're in?
Here, along the riverwalk, after dark
Each failure is its own reward, or nearly,
When one's success is measured by the mouthful
And love lights up like little neon fishes,
God's flashy critics poisoning the blood.

When the Devil Drives

> *The devil is represented with a cloven foot because
> the Rabbinical writers called him* seirizzim *(a goat).*
> —Brewer's Dictionary

I have him stoutly cross-tied in the bed of the truck.
It's twilight. We're speeding down the Interstate.
Passing drivers give Death and the Devil a look
Which might be curiosity or might be hate.
In this green April light we opt for hate.
If the demon in our rear-view is just a goat,
Why does he bleat about his simple fate?
How can he know I plan to slit his rope-burned throat
Almost as soon as we are off the Interstate?
We'll ease over the bridge onto the farm road. I'll wait
For the pines to close in, the dark pines overhead
To muffle with their needles the garbled complaint
About life and death and the God who said
That someone must account for sentimental freight.

In Eclipse

> *How can those terrified vague fingers push*
> *The feathered glory from her loosening thighs?*
> —Yeats

The black river moans. The full moon slips off.
The twisted sycamores give up their hostages
To easy time. She kneels before the latest incarnation
Of the god—her hands upon his golden thighs—
And thinks his flesh is sacred, and thinks the images
Beyond this antic grove are lies. All lies.

Why should lips be vague or fingers terrified
By the flesh they want to hold? Why should love
Last longer than the grunting breath require?
She kneels on dead leaves and begs for him to shove
His flesh past language, beyond the city park,
The river and the trees the red moon sets afire.

God melts like angry words in the wet dark
Of her mouth. A squad car's siren screams
Its long rush past, screams love's failure.
The taste of it explodes in the sound
Of the black river's run, the leaves' cackle,
The great spheres turning themselves around.

Our Lady of the Vapors

Like old aunties reduced to ultimate soul a grey row
Of lockers stiffly overlooks the body of a man just now
Surprisingly dropped to earth. Or maybe magically begotten.
Under the sodden towels the truth is hard and sudden.
The boy in the chainlink cage hangs our keys on the hooks,
Stuffs our wallets in the appropriate pigeon holes and looks
As if he knows just who personifies discretion itself.
We knew, or believed we knew, the source of that laugh
Dancing through the weight room, the steam room, the sauna.
Reginald Jones, Professor of Dance, sweet Reggie Regina—
Our African Queen, our Graham Cracker of dance—
Pranced and strutted his beautiful butt in tight purple pants
Past the muscle-bound lifters at the end of their wits
And the lightweights on steroids pumping up zits . . .
Who? Who? Who? No one knows who did it. No one admits
To killing the best-kept secret of his throbbing heart.
Only one dead faggot, the sergeant says, but it's a start.

Echolalia

The girl kneeling by the pool wants a tongue of fire
To burnish her lips. Her own tongue. Pink
As the lady-slipper's soft petal. Good taste languishes
In the garden's damp loam. Peel back the bulb of desire.
Just one more rank onion. Tongue it. You'll think
Of yourself, your myriad sins, the ill uses language is
Put to when love is put to you like this . . .

A shiver in the ferns at the water's rim—
And then she's left to face her own naked reflection
In the shifty pane where nothing can be trusted
Any more than skin. Your old smile must suffice.
Her grimace is a last displeasure, a leaf's deflection
As it falls into itself and floats there, as grim
As desire itself, killed by what you thought she said.

On Convent Street

No matter the hour she walks her dogs
She meets Major Doppler
On one of his Vietnam jogs
In country. Flailing his arms and legs
He looks like the parts of people dying.
Convent Street, the alley behind her house,
Calls like a bargirl. All the white knights
Lap at her. Nibble, nibble, little mouse.
She giggles. Doppler lies.
Saigon Sally, he says, I love you.
Soldier, she says, you hung like horse.
Through the dark nights
On Convent Street the dreams come flying
Like words with wings, bats after bugs.
On Convent Street everyone flies
Except poor Doppler who jogs
Like a woman in labor,
A liar with a nervous tic.
This is Coke Alley, her backyard,
Where the black folk play with bones
And white folk cruise and Doppler,
Poor Doppler, tries hard
To run backwards, to face the music
Of his own whispers and moans.

In the Locust Grove

Though Birnam Wood be come to Dunsinane...
　　　—Shakespeare

Tomorrow you will find the bruise that is no bruise,
The plum you knew was never yours to eat,
Then Mister Shylock from the bank will call to say
He must foreclose, and you will go to work to learn

That Hamlet and Lear have laughed in one another's arms,
Have called to you and died. But not you yet. Not yet.
Tonight the man at the liquor store said: It will come
Into your cellar after you, lightning will, if it wants you,

And you won't never know it. Listen to the wind, listen
To the goddam wind, hear that cocksucker scream.
You should ask him what the wild air says or whether,
When you leave the porch and let the lightning have it,

You'll have given in to hope or just your fear of death.
Why not sit, wait, and drink your beer? Why not pray?
When the storm clouds break open for a glimpse of sunset,
The newest sentimental observations repeat themselves

Like spring's green leaves made by grey skies greener,
Made gold by lightning bouncing off the clouds of war.
Light clots, grey fibre in a wound, and the colors wail
Across the slice of blue sky, and the black clouds stitch

Themselves together so the storm can go on, a squalling child
Chasing down his murdered brother. Is this proof that Einstein
Didn't make it up—what you claim Turner did? Who knows?
Turner either painted quickly or he remembered everything.

Such art diverts us when we could all be saints or sinners.
Why is the oldest locust last to bloom? Why this spring
Is the lightning so severe? Why are the wrens so fertile
And the nights too mild? Are those bees you hear drowning

In the locust flowers? Is Jesus Christ really the god of death?
A romance hung on twisted trees might be tragedy or farce.
Macduff, the evening smells like honey. All your pretty ones . . .
When the lightning strikes how many dead chicks can you see

In the leaves? How many mad thanes or murdered kings?
Lightning strikes and the trees light up like money
Or revenge, like life and love and hope. And you think, Soon,
Soon I will be free. Yes, soon enough you will be free . . .

A Hole in the Ground of Being

Here's one more Borghesian aleph
On the asphalt path the people tread
Along the riverwalk, one more small hole
To have opened overnight. A breath
Of wind stirred. Rain fell. The river rose.

The black hole, a daemon's bloom
On the dark ground, grew and flourished
Like a black rose against a stone wall
In the Borgias' summer garden.

One man stopping thinks of chance,
Thinks: a slip between bank and lip . . .
And, look here, he might stick his hands
Into this black flower's heart and pull out
A magic harp, a bag of gold.

Or he might be grabbed, he might be
Sucked screaming to the story's end.

The Universal Mall

Mall Rats, Mall Walkers, Tea-Room Queens converge
On Center Court. From here the long arms stretch to take
Whatever space they need. Stiff octopus. Rigid squid.
All motion lies in the molluscan mind's elaboration.
The metaphor of space. Black holes. Wild stellar winds.
Speedy the humped-backed dowager and, in tow,
Her friend, the white-faced man the kids call Shadow, race
Like old cows to the milk parlor, hips jutting, legs pumping,
The chalk bones furious to live. They race, they race
Through Center Court. Under the geodesic dome of the rock.
Down the last lap to the back exit. Past the rest rooms.
They turn and plan to return, eyes down, lest they lose
The line of violet tiles along the middle of the corridor.
Back to the concourse: Head-Start Sears Spenser's Gifts.
Little dogs exhaust their batteries and bare-assed men
Strut their stuffed packages on calendars and birthday cards.
Speedy never wants to look and batty Shadow can't.
But you and I can look. The kids—the mall rats—look
And make a wish on every blown-out well-packed jock.
Again, up and away, they race. Under the glass ceiling,
Past the mirrored panels of the whirling ship, they race.
Above all, visible only from the darkest corners, stars

In an unstitched sampler spin their fishy mockery of speed.
In the men's room two men side by side at the urinals.
And in one stall a boy, no more than a beady eye
At the peep-hole of the wall beside the grappling men,
Their hands crossed, fingers circling one another's cocks.
Even as the one eye glows and, grunting, all three cream,
Flush and go, even as we watch and Speedy humps it
And poor old Shadow grabs his broken heart and flies,
We know what blown nebula is once more lost to dream,
Which stars have burst, and what alarm the darkness cries.

Phantom Pain

What the skulking cat left of the gecko
Still scratches at the back door. Death can't ditch
The remains: the blue tail moves like an echo,
One clawed foot twitches, while the head, as wretched
As a child's nightmare dragon, wants to talk
To the cat's-paw. The lizard's last impression
Draws us out like corpse-lines on the sidewalk.
Don't touch. No balm, no oil, no scented lotion . . .
Don't touch. Let it lie in the leaves and rain,
Smelling of fall, wet ashes in the air.
Don't eat. The gecko's tail might make you blind.
Or give you vivid dreams. Whatever pain
We've guessed is as nothing to the cat's glare,
A gleam like green fire in the gecko's tiny mind.

In the Mail
—A Cargo of Day-old Chicks

At cockcrow we will rise to shrill desire.
There's early morning panic in the coop.
Another gosling suicide, neck like a snake,
Half-fledged, is woven through the fatal wire.
One more day and everyone was home free,
Running with the big birds then, tormenting
The yard dogs, teasing coyotes from the woods.

At the dangerous post office a pair of deranged eyes
Peers through the empty pigeonholes. We wave
And give our half-assed grins. *Hey, man, tell me,*
Is this place safe or should I bring my trusty Uzi in?
Through dark of night, hail of bullets, the true
Appointed rounds—even then the drop dead letter joke
Goes stale and the box of chicks chimes in.

So later, back from riding fence, we find motherhood
In a gloomy mood. The widowed turkey hen
Has hatched her clutch of chicken eggs and the dog
Is mouthing one. Too much of instinct this life requires . . .

A dog will suck an egg. A turkey hen will brood
A clutch of sterile eggs until she starves to death.

Does one rescued dying biddy serve as recompense
So long as it survives to reiterate its pathetic cheep?
Can such a word be understood? What word
Will comprehend the god so angry he has to kill us all?
Recompense for failure? Who has failed to understand
The language of a life both valuable and cheap?

The Teacher Quits

For five more minutes the old teacher lies still, crushed
And wrinkled, as sour as his yellowed sheets and pillows
Where he lives like Gulliver tied down by blood and breath
And consequence. His father's body hangs in the poplar tree
Bursting into bud beyond the window of another dream.
Dead air hardens in the stairwell landing where a group
Of his unhappy students has gathered in his hated name.
He comes upon them standing there, hands to lips, eyes trying
To dice the gray space closing in on them and him.

Echoing words already wander the decades sure to follow
Any awful moment. The students hope they saw him
Just before he heard them curse his stark carping.
They suffer the bitter quotidian of his bankrupt life.
On the wall beside them a sign: DANGER ASBESTOS
HARD HAT AREA. Men in yellow suits, yellow helmets,
Occupy the lobby, discuss their project—to unroll
A giant's condom, to sheathe the building and save a life.

He dreams his cat has sent a figurine crashing from its shelf.
Critical cat. Plaster armadillo, faux bronze from his lost love.
He dumps love's broken body in the trash, the smashed parts

He would rather save than mourn, but nothing can be saved.
Life lapses into junk—his life—and comes crashing down.
Consider glue, witty grimalkin says, not years of a life
Wasted in dusty corners. His father haunts him, reappears
To tell him one September morning on the way to school:
There is no such thing as love. They sit in the old DeSoto
Idling by the ash barrels on the curb while his kitten,
Just run over, dies on the gravel drive behind them,
Thrashes behind them in the wreckage of another day.

The old teacher dreams each night his living father
Dead at ninety-four. He dreams his father younger,
More dangerous as he dies. Nothing sets the teacher free
From the curse of these eternal lives. The other curse
Hangs like his father in the poplar tree outside the window.
He wakes nervous and exhausted, afraid that no one anywhere
Can be sure he loves or is loved. He must face one more day
And fail again to stare it down as he has failed his students,
Tight-lipped on the landing, like witnesses at a grave.

The Word from Marathon

The stoics still come running, these
Mended suicides who believe
Largely in the lungs' wheeze, the grunt

Of faithful effort. Near naked, they weave
In and out of shadow, under the trees
Along the sidewalk where we watch and wave,

Stand and consider. More like trees
Than the trees themselves, we might grant
The worm in the road, the dry leaf,

The high-flying V of Canada geese,
And these—each heart passing, each hopeful self
Who will not pause to cool in the hand's breeze—

A sip from the cup of relief,
If one would breathe the news we want.

April Fool's Day, Morgan Hall
—The Department of English, the University of Alabama, Tuscaloosa Campus

I've risen. I've fed the faithful dogs and noisy parrots,
I've swilled my lovely coffee, checked my e-mail, run
Five righteous miles through the blooming streets
Of Academe, but about suffering I still know nothing.
I've heard that lovers suffer for love, and patriots
For their country, all believers in the fiery test of faith.
After my shower I put on my dead friend's shirt.
On April Fool's Day I fiddle with my taxes
While Rome burns and empirical Tuscaloosa deals
With its sinful park. The fertile world's awash in sin,
The world's a mess. The city's bushhogs howl
In the devastated park and the plaster's falling
Like stars from the ceiling of Morgan Auditorium.
Are these the dead ends of those who will not suffer?
A dead friend's faded Izod shirt? A city clearing out
The bushes wherein the feral cats and faggots hide?
Time stops on April Fool's Day in Morgan Hall.
Time stops. The machine stoppeth. The bloody dogwood,
The velvet pansies, the long-tongued irises refuse to die.
Even the dropping rot in the heart of the hall goes still

For the foolish moment, the gods' ecstatic joke.
Then the clock says tick and the comfortable suffering
Can begin again. Soon, soon enough, the first of May.
Hooray, hooray, the first of May, outdoor fucking . . .
But I forget the rest of the jingle. Whatever was meant
To begin in May will have been overrun by the bushhogs
Or will have withered under the Alabama sun and rain,
While in Morgan Hall the falling plaster sky will prove
That death and taxes are enough to know of pain.
The gilded Greek fretwork was never meant to hold
In place assurances of reality, nor should the world
Out on the street weep at the expected failures of love.

Part Two

EAST HARWICH

Euthanasia

1. Dolphins

Another week of assisted suicides. Late March.
The sounds of spring. The headlines mimic screams.
A school of dolphins is mired in the mudflats
Off of Eastham. They've come ashore to die.
There's a world of comfort in whatever seems
To be the case. With just enough of foam and dune
The photos in our *Capon Islands' News* depict
Stricken volunteers struggling against the mud
The suicidal dolphins wallow in and try to breathe.
In the riddle—black and white and read all over—
The cleaned corpses are sleek as Cadillacs
Parked side by side in the comfortable order
Of the great god Death. Like fifty dead nuns.
Or fifty Balkan refugees. Fifty fingers chopped
Off the dear dancing hands of Shiva. Destroyer?
Preserver? No death is a good death, my dear.

2. Gulls

At our handsome Stop & Shop the shoppers stop
Their shopping for nothing. Not for the headlines.
Not to give the world a hand. Not to watch the gulls
Scavenging the March sky over the Capon Islands.
The gulls forage the garbage bins, the beaches,
The poisoned dump. Their cry is nearly lovely.
Wheeling and screaming above the Stop & Shop
The gulls in one another's eyes aren't dying.
Wire carts roll from fender to bumper to curb.
A cold spring. Trays of pansies, like so many bruises,
Call for the shoppers' attentions. Busy. Noisy.
The old in one another's way can't tell they're old,
Can't read the news: it's spring; we're dying.
It's D-Day on the Capon Islands. It's spring.
Everything that is the case, despite all hopes and plans,
Has conspired to bring us to the beach to die.

Dead Skunk

Lovers on the road are coming and going.
For miles now the sallow moon has been lighting
Them through the musky odor of a death
Already happened. Another of living's
Metaphors, moonlight takes the breath away.
Such black and white the lovers won't believe
Until the last minute, the sudden swerve,
Her cry, his body fluids, their release
Onto the pavement or the leather seats.
So lovers on the road have come and gone.
What else is ever new under the moon?
Nothing, of course. We know that the moon rises
And the dead do not; that the road's next curve—
Like truth from the east—always comes too soon,
A perfume unsettling our frail surmises.

Her Widowed Look

In the frigid air of the Stop & Shop
The Undead prosper. Survival might be
Prosperity. And one hot look might drop
The weakest of them. She has come to buy
Tomorrow's banana. What an optimist!
And a big sack of granite ginger snaps
Just in case the grandchildren come to visit.
And if they do not come—which is likely—
She has cookies enough for Halloween
And Thanksgiving and the drive to Key West
When the frost comes and the air on the Cape
Is colder out than in the Stop & Shop.
What would it take to stop her feeble heart?
A young man's look? An unexpected fart?

Greek Revival Ghost

After midnight, in the back garden, leopard-skin lilies
Open like silk underwear and the cat screams.
Or the neighbor's happy wife. One wonders, one hopes.
Yesterday, Harwich closed the ponds again.
The sun on the water looked just like polio—
Crutches and iron lungs and blank parental fear.
In due time cows will be grazing in Cape Cod Mall.
The ghosts—the bones and hides and yellow teeth—
Shimmer in the heat that chases the cars around
The rotary, chases them up and over the bridge,
Chases them down the last unpaved sandy lane,
Past the scrub oak and scrub pine and beach roses . . .

At noon the Regulator clock chimed once and died.
The radio shifted stations. No more news.
Then the whole house shook—a kind of *frisson*—
As if the house at last remembered something.
Hurricane season. The summer people flee, the old
And rich, the young and lovely. They want to live forever!
Hurricane season. The summer drones, the wind
At night beheads the silky lilies, someone cries.
Don't hurt me, Daddy! This might be ecstasy or pain,

The wind or the neighbor's cat in summer heat
Or in the mouth of a coyote. The wild kingdom
Plays out on a screen of wind-whipped fog.

Yesterday at breakfast and then again at bedtime
The wind, like heavy footsteps, rumbled through
The garret room above the kitchen, the oldest part
Of the house—where a ghost might be, the ghost
One gets for always having wanted to be haunted.
Now that he's here, what's his point? His plan?
To drive the living out? To make an old wrong right?
To prove he has the prior claim to this old place?
Does he want company or want to be alone?
Come winter, when the chill wind bites and the air
Is full of ice, he'll want the softer, warmer bed
And, in exchange, he'll offer his one cold kiss.

Salt Water Taffy

Who told her this silence would save her soul?
Cobwebs grow in kitchen corners, in all
The corners, and across the lawn a skein
Of fog blows like a dead bride's veil, and out
On the road the summer people pass through
Her ken like mosquitoes through the torn screens.
Or did she think sweetness would save her soul?
If this candy is not enough to fill
Her mouth and drown her tongue, she has a crock
Of salt and a bag of sand and bad news
She'll have to repeat once she's cleared her throat.
On Monomoy, dogs are eating the terns.
Terns in Provincetown are eating the dogs.
Are turned words the secret which saves her soul?
Becalmed for the summer, she watches fog
Roll through her windows. Fog muffles the note
Of discord—the hint of dismay—the croak
Of the bird stuffed in the back of her throat.

Indian Summer in the Capon Islands

Fat black flies as big as gumdrops appear
Out of nowhere to buzz from pane to pane.
Open the window, they stay, canaries
Of the false fall, fallen angels who pine
For winter, souls who have nothing to fear
At the feast of . . . here, in the fiefdom of . . .
At the bony feet of the great god death.
From sure perches near their redundant feeder
Fat titmice, cardinals and chickadees
Return through glass the look of stale provender.
Flies buzz. Birds quarrel. One of us considers
The end of time: the jet stream's out of breath,
Or the Gulf Stream's off its course, but of course
All that's wrong really is this dreary light.

On Red River Beach

The breeze dies. Nantucket Sound lies as nigh
As God before the first demented thought
Turned light and color into words apart.
Back and forth, end to end, we who would live
Forever walk the shore road parking lot.
In the dunes the wharf rats breed and their young
Outlive us, lost in our last brilliant dream.
Sic Transit comics call the hospice bus.
Bracketed by hurricanes, these fall days
Tease American light from the bright sky.
Up in Boston the Sargent show has closed
At last, while on the Cape the kales and mums
Provide a chilled image of eternal life.
On the beach at sunset one more day labors
Like an iron lung. Hush, hush, the sea soughs
In its struggle against the granite groins
The State built to keep safe the doctor's manor.
Today the seaweed smells like iodine.
If he weren't already safe on his boat
In the Keys, the good doctor would be pissed.

Halloween

When at last the sleet began to strike
My window, I pulled back. Ice shattered
Itself as if it could destroy the reflecting glass
And me behind it. Ice soon greased each spike
Of the black fence, each delinquent leaf in a battery
Of bleared hope, cruel Christ's bright and suffocating mass.
Against my tongue the parlor window stuck like ice.
Against my eyes the cold panes wore a smudge
Of lips, my name erased, a grillwork lace
Of tic-tac-toe rubbed out. Could I begrudge
God's wrath its weather? Rain should have been blood,
Red fog on the moon, not His wet ghost climbing
From the graveyard to fill my cold childhood
With a face like my own, glaring through the skull of time.

Sunset Strip

At Red River Beach the season runs down.
On one another's arms the old patrol
The parking lot—back and forth, back and forth—
Looking for the exit. A black-backed gull
Screeches from its roost on the restroom roof.
The last summer people chase desperate pleasure—
Breaker, shell, ball or breath—across cold sand.
Perched on the power pole above the dune
A big bird without the proper papers waits
To be identified. Not *Youngblood Hawk*
Or *Flight of Eagles* or *The Maltese Falcon*,
But the buzzard come to take our measure.
Gritty days at the beach grind to a halt
Under the bleak gaze of his hungry eye.

After a Life of Art

At last, November. And so the bronze oak
Should shed and the young man roofing the house
Across the street should not be nearly nude
Or as bronze as these leathery old leaves.
In Eden naked Adam owned no house,
Had no need of shingles, no shirtless man
Whose smooth skin seen through the dry leaves might prove
The future rougher than the angel's word.
Like Sistine Adam reaching for a can
Of nails the young man opposite has stretched
His muscled charm across the dome of time.
In Milton's Neighborhood a happy tree
Would blossom, bear, and drop its fruit at once
Straight into Winter's crabbed arthritic hand.

Snow Sculpture

The unfinished house squats over a field of snow.
Memory is naked and it hisses like a red hot poker
Thrust into another little scene by Currier and Ives.
Tommy is a friend of mine, he will blow me any time . . .
What could be the occasion of a molten poker
Briefly steaming in a snowman's snowball ass?
Everyone in a white nightmare has hot coals for eyes.
Tommy is a friend of mine, he will blow me any time,
For a nickel, for a dime, fifteen cents for overtime.
A scaffold of yellow pine loses its color in the cold.
Twilight. A pack of wild boys yelling, running circles
Around the hollow house. They build a trash fire.
They bring to bay, beyond their arms' reach,
Another boy who has stacked against his pain—
In the drifted attic, among the gray studs and rafters—
Scrap lumber and snowballs packed with nails.
Tommy is a friend of mine, he will blow me any time . . .
Near the fire a six-foot phallus sculpted of snow.
The boys hurl their own icy weapons almost far enough.
At the edge of the field Napoleon's white war horse

Rears and prances and tramples the blue snow.
Hitler's panzers stall in the ice around Leningrad.
The wolf pack howls anger, howls pain, one by one—
For a nickel, for a dime, fifteen cents for overtime—
From the attic, one by one, the boys retreat,
Gone, out of hearing, off the edge of the burnt page,
Carrying away with them the mingled smells
Of cold semen and scorched paint, carrying away
Into next summer's underbrush their little song:
Tommy is a friend of mine, he will blow me anytime,
For a nickel, for a dime, fifteen cents for overtime.
Everything remains forever unfinished, unforgiven,
Everything stalled in the drifting snow and smoke.

The Capon Islands' News

They hardly matter—Mister Toad or Mister Hedgehog
Chopped by the John Deere, or little Bambi run down
By the Ford Explorer, or Peter Rabbit together with
Flopsy, Mopsy and Cottontail, all four bunnies impaled
On mercy's spear. Or if the Magic Kingdom really matters
Almost as much as money, love and fame, if they aren't
All the same thing, if they might really weigh on the road
Home from Disney World, the trudge upstairs to bed,
Who's left who cares to say? So much huffing and puffing
Won't blow nobody's house down. Today on the beach road
A sad freight of sentiment again bent the Clydesdales' backs
Under an unkind load: one more dead pig and a spider
Crying over it. What did her tears claim? The language
Of the passing world? What's that worth? What does it matter
That nothing's real and that Charlotte hates us till the end of time?

Positively Elizabethan

> *Look in thy glass and tell the face thou viewest...*
> —Shakespeare

To be told he's spent too much of his life
Conflating sex and death in poetry
Might make a queer man feel positively
Elizabethan. Gay, my dear, and then some.
You meet a famous gay star at a soiree.
He is sixty-three and still so handsome
You have to ask him what his diet is.
A lover, he says, who looks as I looked
When I was only twenty. This boy here.
The next day you see at a reunion
A man who, at seventeen, might have been
A Greek god—had you believed in Greek gods.
At fifty-six he's now the world's cliché
For fat, bald, bearded, rapacious and mean.
His son asks what his father had been like
As a boy. He was amazing, you say.
You do not say the man had always been mean.
You say he was handsome and more than smart.
Idols were what you called sex objects then.
He'd been an idol and he's come to dust,

But this could not be said to his fine son,
Not yet bald, still trying to be the best
Of all the boys. That you were merely dirt
Under his father's feet could not be said.
That then or now one could crush your queer head
Beneath the handsome heel could not be said.
Your father still had hair, is what you say.
Will the truth eventually sound true?
Beauty is its own humiliation
And men become the dead they have for lunch.
The unasked question for the movie star:
Were he a dentist or a plastic surgeon
Would crowned teeth and facelifts still foster love?
This loving son is your dark confessional
Where you whisper that sex and death are gifts.
But the moment is too conditional
And his beauty really is a bridge too far.

Deer in the Headlights

They want celebration, the critics do,
Not reminders of what the world is like—
Like the doe, as frail as charity, who
One night is standing in the roadway as if
She knows we have to stop or at least slow
Our inevitable progress to take a look
At raptured nature. For just one whiff
Of the wild pelt we interrupt the need
Which brings her here to dare her death like this.
How could a critic ever comprehend
Traffic bearing down on a lover's kiss?
Brakes scream. Like magic the doe disappears
Into the hedgerow. Gone, all hopes and fears,
Dispelled like dust by such a happy end.

Snapdragons, Et Cetera

Go now, my friend, and you'll miss the lilacs.
If you wait a week, you'll see the poppies
And then the rhododendrons. You can't go then,
Not with weeks of roses promising the summer
Perfume and light, then every day the daylilies
Coming and going in a frenzy of lost souls.
Today the locusts fill the space between earth
And our dream of heaven. Snakes in the garden,
They stand on their tails, heads in the clouds.
The Masque is *Spring*—in Japanese contortions—
The serpent disguised as his suffering tree—
The huge delicacy of locust leaf and honey flower—
Orioles swaying in those fragile topmost boughs.

Go now; you'll miss the coyote coming tonight
For the cat hunting the mouse, the mouse and his bit
Of grain caught in the owl's eye. You'll miss
The smell of honeysuckle, the lambent moon,
The garden's lunacy. But if you stay, you'll find
In the morning, in the damp humus, the prints
Of the deer that raided the green corn; you'll see

The bit of fur and blood caught on the barbwire,
The vast clear blue sky and the dry eye of one
Who woke and found he was not left behind.
If you stay. Though, God knows, you do not have to.
Still, you planted words; you might hope to reap
Your fragrant promises, our love's delicious lies.

Part Three

TUAM

Beyond Nantucket

Beyond Nantucket the world lies waiting.
Seas rage and the universe flattens out.
Who'd have guessed there really was an edge
And that in our madness we might fall off?
Could anyone have foreseen the Irish craze
For life-size plaster statues of Oliver Hardy?
Who stuck the crosier in the crook of his arm?
Who do that Voodoo that you do so well?
Another pope lies dying and dying lies
About the Fascists' love of humor.
Something offshore glows like a world afire,
Another world, better by far than this.
And yet any fool knows what is
And is not so. So much for desire.
Nothing makes sense this close to the sea.
The currents sweep north-northeast,
Warm water moving like a snake
Through the cold Atlantic. Deep beneath
The surface drowned sailors, foolish men
Who yearned for grace and blubber,

Must have found their subtext wanting.
What is humor? Hubris? The light turning
Cockleshells green? Who wants to die?
Who wants to live forever? The fish eye
Staring in the grocer's case . . . You see,
The language is nothing but your yearning
To play a joke on God, another toothy fish
Staring sidewise from the grocer's case.
Perhaps you really meant the *starring* gar.
In any case, fisheye is a kind of lens
For deforming the world. Look down.
See the starfish, as big as dinner plates?
They're telling one another ethnic jokes.
In Haiti, Saint Patrick represents Dambala,
The God of Gods, whose symbol
Is the wee green snake. There are no snakes
In Ireland, no rabies and no saints.
There's Oliver Hardy staring out to sea,
Contemplating the dead man's float.
Back to Nantucket. The long way round.
Go now. Before the universe flattens out.

The Beasts of Coole Park

Their hearts have not grown old...
—Yeats

Like a wolf with wings I will circle back
Through a wet December dawn to the deer
Racing the high walls of their asylum.
These survive: the two does and the buck,
The green silence, the soft rain, and the fear
Like the ghost of a house where not one room
Still stands and none of those whose words could break
The wild heart still lives to open a door,
To breathe one bright syllable of welcome.
Like a wolf with wings I have circled back
Through the empty park to the frightened deer.
Their wild eyes bleed and scream, their wild hearts drum
Like great wings beating still, like the white birds
Who could bring back dead souls or lovely words
Were madness merely a matter of will.

Opera Queens

No news is good news. The headline: NO NEWS TODAY.
In the ever-present now the same stars burst over Colchis,
Thessaly, Athens, the same stars fall on Belfast and Atlanta,
The same radical pink dactyls reach for the sky at dawn
In the moment that never changes and changes everyone.
From the Punchbowl in Park Square, Boston, doomed queens—
La vie en rose—emerge into the gray false dawn to sing
These monodies. *Tosca. Aïda. La Boheme. La Traviata.*
Mad, sad Medea, dearest mother of us all, pray, sweetie, pray.
There is always, is there not, the present moment, madam?
The poet said the giggling Greeks are dancing cheek to cheek
And the foul-mouthed French are on their knees in the garden.
Because of her great sacrifice, the pains that split her open,
Mother sits knitting, knitting another queer fate to fit us,
To wrap us up, as she is wrapped, in the twisted yarn
Of her desires. Mommy dearest, Mimi Defarge, Medea.
The blue globe balled like a fist in the folds of her lap,
She knows she is the ever-present now that owns us all.
Mother Courage Mother May I Mother Mary Shall It Be?
There is always the present moment. At the cash register
Bold type screams the news: JASON DUMPS MEDEA.
In the checkout line we scan the photos, examine the text.

Magical Medea, her serpents harnessed, her babies strapped
To the chariot's hubs, drives down to the shivery Thracian sea.
Near dawn the Punchbowl empties out its bilge of soggy fruits.
She's one more bitter queen left in the lurch by a fickle man,
One more pissed-off mother who will not take it lying down
Or up her ass or on her knees, never again in any of the ways
She once mistook for love. She'll run him down, mad Medea,
She'll make him pay, that fleecing bastard, the dirty prick,
The father of us all. She is always fleeing Colchis, the wrath
Of Aetes, another stupid father, stupid king in hot pursuit . . .
Of what? The honeymooning couple? That precious fleece?
Out of the flying ship she threw her brother's heart and head.
Here, Daddy, his arms, his legs, and this, this little dangle
Of your generations yet to come that will not come from him.
Aetes stops to gather up the floating pieces of Absyrtus . . .
In Park Square, in the men's room of the Greyhound Station,
From the overflowing urinals, from the sticky yellow tiles.
Medea goes overboard, back to Thessaly, on to Athens,
Her last aria fading as she goes. The driverless chariot sinks,
Serpents slipped from their traces, the babies tied to the hubs,
The babies drowning, waving in the cold sea arms and legs
Like kelp on the dark currents, and letting loose the gasp
Of surprise, the last burbles of protest, the bubbly cries
Of one old queen, head in the toilet, asking the water why.

Two Lips to Die For

Like the dying summer our poor old mad God
Has a hard-on for some breathing flesh,
A pair of lips, a pretty little kiss, a piece,
A little piece of ass to carry him through to spring.
Poor priapic God. Even with the biggest dick of all
He needs a Porsche to be sure of scoring.

Amphibia's emperies, the brilliant poet wrote,
Who knew perhaps that in such absolute dominions
Amphibians guarded their warm hearts and soft lips.
In the movie of our lost youth, Death's lips are full
And split and look like bruised wet mucous membranes.
Not at all like fruit, despite Death's pretensions.

I must remember to tell the poet he got it right
About the toads, dropped here by aliens,
And now they're disappearing, going home
With what they've learned, for what it's worth,
Before our planet pops like a ripened zit.
Can we miss what we haven't learned to love?

Death would have us all believe his penis is for peeing.
That his lips are targets for the old and sick at heart.

At Columcille's Well
—County Donegal

Up here I can think of nothing good I should want to cure
Except life itself—which, of course, means death.
Nonetheless I empty a vitamin jar of its few futile pills
And fill it with water for my faithful American mother.
Below is the road back to Galway, each mile farther
From the war of the saints who trouble us all.
On the dual carriageway a military convoy takes care
That swiftly, safely, Ireland's money move from here to there.
I suffer in ignorance such relative words, while under the hills
My dead cousins' bones fight to reformulate breath.
I stand on the ruin of Columcille's hill—abbey and well,
Relics and cattle and asphalt and space—a hell of a view,
Too lovely for mortals, too distant for mortals to love.
Back in Gortahork the parish priest has fixed his curse
On a poet who's admitted he's gay. Aren't we all?
Don't you wake every morning with a mark on your brow?
Embroidered by fairies, a six-pointed star on your sleeve?
In the days when other folk starved, a priest would have kept
A sheep or a pig or even a cow in a pen by his parish hall.
The priest of this curse keeps in his graveyard a peacock,
The kind of pride you can buy for a penny or two,

Two harps and a Guinness. The priest tells the poet to die.
On Columcille's roofless altar, under the savage sky,
Pilgrims leave coins and feathers, whisky, spittle and blood;
They leave what they should, they look at the sky, at the valley,
At the mountains around them, they grieve for the holy,
And then they depart, having touched as much of the world
As they could. For revenge I wanted the peacock to die,
To turn back the ignorant curse and prove nothing
But my own regret. Death comes too soon for peacock
And priest, even in Gortahork where the saints are skewed,
Where a peacock is worth more than a priest. And yet—
As in English we say of some beauties—the countryside here
Is to die for. Running from pagans, Saint Columcille's mother
Changed with the blood of Columcille's birth the clay
Of this mountain from blood red to bone. She changed
The story of the valley from merely scenic to nearly true.
In Irish it might well have been true. Then mothers and poets
And peacocks had souls. We should pray for the priest
Who deserves less than what this sprinkle of water might do.
Consider the well on the hillside, the transubstantial view:
The well offers up chrism and wine, jissom, spittle or blood.
Whatever fluid he drinks, like us he is wholly deranged . . .
Dying forever, caught in the hell of his own understanding,
Thinking in Irish, having forgotten the English for you,
The priest must dispute with us all what it means to be good.

When Irish Eyes Are Smiling

The new gate goes here, despite the rain turning
My hard dug dirt to muck. Work must be done
Or else another day is lost to dreaming.
Their eyes, he said, *their ancient glittering eyes* . . .
But what did he know? When did he go down
On his knees and crawl under the cold eyes
Of a man whose look did more than seem
To promise love? Dig out another stone
And lay it where the wall might one day rise
To block my view of life's temptations burning
On green horizons made of rain and stone.
I'll refence the field once the gate is done,
I'll stack the turf, and then I'll go to town
To drink a pint to eyes that set me dreaming.

Articles of Faith
—My Mother, the Pope and the Other Woman

Because all things on earth must have a name,
This room in which my mother meets the pope
Is called . . . Pomerania, the Chapel Perilous, Pa-Moo.
Because I have the photographic record of a moment
My mother plans to send as next year's Christmas card,
I have been granted a chance on all tomorrow's truth.
Because everything on earth must have a name,
She is Mother, he is Carol Wotiya, alias John Paul,
And the other woman—dressed in a smock whiter
Than the pope's—is called, for now, the other woman.
This room in which my mother meets the pope
Is lined with tall dark books bound in leather,
Embossed in gold with the changing names of truth.
My mother holds the pope's right hand in both of hers.
She speaks. She is so old we cannot tell she smiles.
They are facing one another, my mother and the pope,
But only she is looking. Jesus' eyes turn sadly inward
That he might better understand the words he hears.
(Or maybe he looks down at the well-stuffed Polish self.)
A multi-lighted chandelier shines like an excessive halo

Directly over the head of the interposing other woman
Standing in the near background, in the space between
The happy couple, that space reserved for two seraphim,
Tall as two Swiss Guards and fierce in the face of love.
Because all things on earth must have some sort of name.

Last Will and Testament

The lovely tedium of cloud and song
Calls the sad soul home. I'll ask how you're keeping—
Tin whistle at the ready, rain hat donned.
You'll frown to hear my easy Irish tongue,
My newfound guff, the sounds of fall seeping
Into the wet evening. *Why wouldn't I
Keep well?* you'll ask, your restless eyes sweeping
The cottage clear of dust, the farmyard free
Of weeds and chickens, all my lazy trash.
They live like pigs, you'll say, *and drive like rats*,
Your mind still racing through the maze of roads,
The muck and ruts between the high stone walls,
Shannon to Tuam and down my narrow lane.
Our first meeting, then, since our father died
Back in America where no one dies
But by accident or misadventure,
Where the sun shines always and life is sure.
I'll light the stove, reheat a pot of stew,
And while we eat you'll tell me what is new
Back home, though this is home, this cottage where

I've come to rest apart from love and pain.
Later we shall sit and talk before the fire
And maybe you will play an air or two,
Though I shan't dance the reels of your desire.
Gouge out your eyes, or keen and tear your hair—
You will have brought a gift of grief and guilt
I will not open. Wind and rain will lash
The cracked windows, the turf will glow and smoke,
And I shall smoke, and you will disapprove.
We might sit this way till the rooster crows
And another wet day breaks around us.
I did not love him. You, my brother, did.
Those words of woe we'll have to leave unsaid.

Orpheus at the River

All these years and still his brain will recoil,
As mute thought rebels, against the edict:
A poet found wandering the high roads
Shall be stripped of lute and pen and the name
Of the unspeakable god shall be tattooed
Across his breast. Thenceforth the snake he wore
Flicked at one small nipple a tongue like teeth.
He was beheaded, his body left nude,
Skinned nearly raw, simulacrum removed,
Mere blackened meat to feed the Thracian crows.
Legless drunk all these centuries of turmoil,
Like flotsam his head tossed from whore to whore,
He loses in this game all sense of who
She was and why he sang for her before
The darkness and the thoughtful silence came.

The Bones of Temple Jarlath

> *. . . there you shall build your oratory, for God wills that there shall be the place of your resurrection, and many shall arise in glory in the same place along with you.*
>
> —St. Brendan the Navigator

In Tuam, in the west of Ireland, the wheel
Of Jarlath's chariot broke, as Brendan, not yet
A saint, had foretold, so Jarlath hitched his ass
To the wreck and, as my friend Sean Walsh has said,
Went into Gilligans for a pint. History is the rest:
A great cathedral, now Protestant, and the sacred
School of Tuam, which sounds like *tomb* and should.
Young Brendan sent Jarlath two miles to the east
While he, the navigator in his ox-hide boat, sailed west—
Beyond the whale-road—to find for Holy Ireland America
And all that *lebensraum* the world could do without.
Meanwhile, back in Tuam, a drunk has made his home
In a tomb in Temple Jarlath. And aren't the pubs abuzz
With the scandal of his desperate measures!
Because there was room, he said, for only one to sleep,
He took the long yellow bones and the toothy skull,
The fragile fingers and toes, vertebrae and broken ribs,

And dumped them in a skip. The relics lost. Lost!
Or would be, had they been Jarlath's bones, those bones,
Those dry bones encased in silver and "translated"
In 1415 to *Teampul na scrin* beside the great cathedral.
So the town has found one drunk a proper house as well.
In Gilligans we shake our woozy heads. A house for him
To wreck and not pay rent, to burn the doors and floors
Against the coming winter's cold. Just to ease our souls.
Yet who can account for the miracle? It's been three days
And our holy drunk is sober, in a tie and drinking milk.
Sure, it won't last, says Sean, who offered him a job
Digging potatoes. *Let the fucker who hid them find them*,
Is what the saint said. *Best to say nothing*, Sean said.
Aye, said the doctor, *and keep on saying it*. Which might do,
If it weren't for the missing bones and the miracle.

Home on the Range

Today, above the highland bog, above the wet plateau,
The spinning sun dropped off behind dark clouds.
The color spread—dirty pink,
What one high-toned Boston mother called old rose:
She took a pint of blood, a lump of coal . . .
Really, that was how she made her palette sing,
Her roughrider cup his balls and, cupping, squeeze.
But not too hard. The thick clouds roll and roll.
This cowboy says he's sorry, he doesn't think
He is the man for her, little thing, puny ancient thing,
Thin lipped and breastless, weak eyes, purple nose . . .
The blood dark face drawn out of the roiling clouds
Loves to prove my point: narcissism is a cruel disease;
Old, and the uglier we get, the more difficult to please.

The House of Dreams

Undress downtown, in the dark, at the RKO Paramount,
Amidst a decor dripping with gilt and red velvet.
Wide staircases curve past hugely tearful chandeliers.
Steps rise almost imperceptibly to those balconies round
As shells and each aglow with the pearl of Mother's presence.
See, up there, a blue-eyed Apache crawls through a patch of corn.
Over and over, ugly old cross-eyed Geronimo
Is changed, as you are changed and I am changed, changed utterly
By one desire. You are fourteen, naked, foolish and afraid
Of any man who might laugh your blue-eyed Indian
To scorn, or worse, who might laugh you both into the joke,
The handshake, the look between you, intimacy meant
To exclude his wife, your rival, and his son, your friend.
How's your blue-eyed Indian today? he will slyly ask
And look you slowly up and down as if you have concealed
About your person the handsome fakery, the gilt and velvet,
Of the dyed and costumed man who plays Geronimo
While you, dark-eyed and scrawny, feel more the part.
All men scare you, all men and older boys, whose touch
Means pain, whose skin is rough and dangerous, whose kiss . . .

Until he touches you, you have no proof of love, no passion
Or obsession, no sense more real than vague dreams
And sinful fears of a man's body overtaking yours.
At the Fairmont James Dean poses naked for you.
Montgomery Clift gallops naked through the Oriental.
Tall princes abrade themselves in the palaces of dreams.
The ceilings come with stars and sweet clouds drift
Above the beams of colored light in glad transfiguration . . .
In the Paramount and Fairmont, the Oriental, the Gaiety,
You find out who you are and what it is you've wanted.

The Broken Tower

1. The First Sunday of Advent

The view proliferates now that the leaves
Have fallen—ash and oak stripped of their gold
By the wind which, we are told, loves nothing
But itself and cold rain. The Clare has risen
Like a full heart to flood the valley below
My house. From the new islands the sheep call.
My friends have decided I want a wife
To keep me company over the Christmas.
Then what? Better to save the stranded ewes—
One at a time—than consider a life
Surrendered to views of shattered beauty.
With winter the round tower at Kilbannon
Rises headless across the river valley.
Another past without a present point,
Stones scattered like the monks' dreams of safety.
Norsemen find the ladder raised and the gold—
Like God—risen out of reach. The siege begins.
Stones fall into the tall grass. Tourists come

With cameras to gather the lost booty.
Last night Saint Jarlath carried the sheep across
The river. Saint Brendan navigated.
The wind howled and the rain lashed the bare trees.
Who could be lonely among these glad ghosts?
Like candles they glimmer outside my windows.

2. Christmas Eve

The new fireplace in the sitting room waits
For the mortar to dry. The night's so still
I can hear the sheep bleating in the meadow.
Not a breath of wind to blame for the banshee
In the chimney or the tap at the window.
Today at the broken tower I mistook
The lichen on the stones for Celtic scrolls,
Whorled like snails, the last words of ruined monks.
This morning I read of a duck named Maeve,
Record layer of the world's largest egg.
She's a local duck living on her fame
In Belclare, just a few miles down the road.
By Guinness, Queen Maeve and her golden egg

Are the gospel truth, like Kilbannon's stones.
Under the grass, the dead writhe like mud snails
Working their slow way through the jealous flesh.
My flesh is jealous too. The cold panes sweat.
Stille Nacht. The stars could be contraband
In the black sky above Kilbannon church
Where conflagrations light the brain and heart.
The first flames in the new fireplace will send
My ghost up the dark chimney and out
Among the swirling others who have found
No peace on earth and no release from heaven.

Wren Hunting
—The Bog above Spiddal,
Connemara, Christmas Day

Up here the tumbled ancestral house proves the Irish are mad.
Like loose cows their names have scattered. Their stones are driven
To pasture on the open bog. One seeks an account in the Irish words
For why and what, who and where, mother, father, death and pride.

Up here the pointless dead run wild, although no one sees them.
And who knows to say that the screaming black and white crows
Are magpie nuns? When the wren-killing boys come to the door,
What will suffice to settle the score of Saint Stephen's Day?

Up here the wind strips a man to the bones he thought flesh clad.
The boy on the road—blue-eyed, black-haired boy—is he forgiven
For turning back the look in his eyes, cryptic as these bogland birds?
Not a one of them sees him. Not a one of them even looks aside.

Up here, on the frozen bogs above Spiddal, the cold soul cries, I am,
And sounds like any raven or magpie, cawing the pissed fool's, no! no!
Free to sing her songs to the wind, the Old World wren cannot soar,
Nor does she care that she be worth the penny paid tomorrow.

Sweet Afton

> *Flow gently, Sweet Afton, among they green braes,*
> *Flow gently, I'll sing thee a song in thy praise.*
> —Burns

Snow today, so wet and white the new lambs
Across the lane look like small clots of smoke,
Grim as the hooks on which they'll someday hang.
I guess that life in any lane, even here
In Holy Ireland, is sprinkled with the crumbs
Of consolation. Some destined to choke
On the blood pumping from their own slit throats
Don't know the lamentations they should sing,
While others have been warned of what to fear.
My pack of cigarettes—ten little smokes—
Is inscribed with poetry and death threats.
Smug as the weather beating down the sheep,
One could study the snow turning to sleet,
The wind shredding itself in the blackthorns,
Ewes and lambs huddled against the stone walls,
And find in the silence the text of things
Beyond the window and across the lane.

The day melts into whiskey and cigarettes.
The radio plays. Turf burns in the stove.
Serenity might be things going on
While Lyric FM celebrates Charles Ives,
One more American insurance man,
Seller of the silence that is not there
And the silence that is. The dark roar
Of wind in the chimney adds its dissonance
To notes from elsewhere. Between intervals
The fist of the wind raps at the wet door.
Outside, the lambs bleat and the cold rain falls
Into the black waves of the River Clare.

Envoi

Epimetheus
—after "Stone Man" by Barbara Kline

In the garden, among the withered vines,
Naked and nameless on a cold stone bench,
I waited for my new life to begin—
Like a musical comedy—*One Touch*
Of Venus—and love's kiss would set me free.
Through the long night I imagined sweet crimes
Against nature, what the priests have called sin,
But all those hours no one came to save me.
To be stone and yet ungrounded in a fog
Of regret . . . hammered and chiselled by longing . . .
Suppose I had spared Medusa, not stuck
Narcissus, let Ulysses be a hog . . . ?
Not earth. Not heaven. Just the clouds' grey song,
Thought turning into flesh, flesh into rock.

About the Author

Thomas Rabbitt was born in Boston and educated at the Boston Latin School and Harvard College. From 1972 until 1998 he taught at the University of Alabama in Tuscaloosa. He now lives on a farm in the west of Ireland.

Rabbitt's work has appeared in many publications (among them *The Nation*, *Poetry*, and *Esquire*) and has been often anthologized (recently in *Best American Poetry 2000*, *The Pushcart Prize XIX*, *Buck and Wing*, and *The Ohio Review: New and Selected*). He won the Pitt Prize for his first book and has been awarded fellowships from the National Endowment for the Arts and the Alabama Council on the Arts. *Prepositional Heaven* is his ninth collection.